50 =Dishes for a Perfect Picnic

By: Kelly Johnson

Table of Contents

- Caprese Salad
- Chicken Salad Sandwiches
- Pasta Salad
- Grilled Veggie Skewers
- Deviled Eggs
- Hummus and Pita Bread
- Fruit Salad
- Cheese and Charcuterie Board
- Quinoa Salad
- Antipasto Skewers
- Tuna Salad Wraps
- Watermelon Feta Salad
- Shrimp Cocktail
- Cold Fried Chicken
- Veggie Spring Rolls
- Pimento Cheese Spread
- Cucumber Sandwiches
- Tomato and Mozzarella Skewers
- Roasted Chickpeas
- Sweet Potato Salad
- Mini BLT Sandwiches
- Grilled Chicken Skewers
- Mediterranean Couscous Salad
- Roasted Red Pepper Dip
- Stuffed Mini Peppers
- Guacamole and Chips
- Spinach and Cheese Stuffed Croissants
- Bacon-Wrapped Dates
- Cabbage Slaw
- Corn on the Cob
- Veggie Wraps
- Grilled Cheese Sandwiches
- Fresh Bruschetta
- Chocolate Chip Cookies
- Lemon Bars

- Picnic-Style Potato Salad
- Turkey and Cheese Roll-ups
- Sweet and Sour Meatballs
- Marinated Olives
- Fruit Tart
- Roasted Potato Wedges
- Zucchini Fritters
- Sliced Cold Cuts and Pickles
- Roasted Cauliflower Salad
- Mini Meatball Subs
- Spinach and Ricotta Puffs
- Cantaloupe and Prosciutto
- Brownie Bites
- Sliced Brie and Grapes
- Iced Lemonade

Caprese Salad

Ingredients:

- 4 ripe tomatoes, sliced
- 8 oz fresh mozzarella cheese, sliced
- 1/4 cup fresh basil leaves
- 2 tbsp extra virgin olive oil
- 1 tbsp balsamic vinegar (optional)
- Salt and freshly ground black pepper, to taste

Instructions:

1. **Prepare the Ingredients:** Slice the tomatoes and mozzarella cheese into even slices. Tear the basil leaves into smaller pieces if needed.
2. **Assemble the Salad:** On a large platter, arrange the tomato slices, mozzarella slices, and basil leaves in an alternating pattern, slightly overlapping.
3. **Season the Salad:** Drizzle the extra virgin olive oil over the salad, and if desired, drizzle a bit of balsamic vinegar on top for added flavor.
4. **Finish and Serve:** Sprinkle with a pinch of salt and freshly ground black pepper to taste. Serve immediately as a refreshing appetizer or side dish.

Chicken Salad Sandwiches

Ingredients:

- 2 cups cooked chicken breast, shredded
- 1/2 cup mayonnaise
- 1 tbsp Dijon mustard
- 1/4 cup finely chopped celery
- 1/4 cup finely chopped red onion
- Salt and freshly ground black pepper, to taste
- 4 slices whole wheat or white bread
- Lettuce leaves (optional)

Instructions:

1. **Prepare the Chicken Salad:** In a bowl, combine shredded chicken, mayonnaise, mustard, celery, and onion. Mix well.
2. **Season:** Add salt and pepper to taste.
3. **Assemble the Sandwich:** Spread the chicken salad mixture onto two slices of bread. Optionally, add lettuce leaves before closing the sandwich.
4. **Serve:** Slice the sandwich and serve immediately.

Pasta Salad

Ingredients:

- 2 cups cooked pasta (penne, rotini, or your favorite shape)
- 1/2 cup cherry tomatoes, halved
- 1/4 cup diced cucumber
- 1/4 cup diced red bell pepper
- 1/4 cup sliced black olives
- 1/4 cup crumbled feta cheese
- 1/4 cup Italian dressing
- Salt and pepper to taste

Instructions:

1. **Prepare the Vegetables:** Chop the tomatoes, cucumber, bell pepper, and olives.
2. **Combine:** In a large bowl, mix the cooked pasta with the chopped vegetables and feta cheese.
3. **Dress the Salad:** Pour the Italian dressing over the pasta mixture and toss to coat.
4. **Serve:** Season with salt and pepper, then chill before serving for best flavor.

Grilled Veggie Skewers

Ingredients:

- 1 zucchini, sliced into rounds
- 1 red bell pepper, cut into chunks
- 1 yellow bell pepper, cut into chunks
- 1 red onion, cut into chunks
- 8 oz cherry tomatoes
- 2 tbsp olive oil
- 1 tsp dried oregano
- Salt and pepper, to taste

Instructions:

1. **Prepare the Veggies:** Thread the zucchini, bell peppers, onion, and cherry tomatoes onto skewers.
2. **Season:** Drizzle olive oil over the veggies, then sprinkle with oregano, salt, and pepper.
3. **Grill:** Grill the skewers over medium-high heat for 6-8 minutes, turning occasionally until the veggies are tender and lightly charred.
4. **Serve:** Remove from the grill and serve warm.

Deviled Eggs

Ingredients:

- 6 large eggs, hard-boiled and peeled
- 3 tbsp mayonnaise
- 1 tsp Dijon mustard
- 1 tbsp pickle relish
- Salt and pepper, to taste
- Paprika, for garnish

Instructions:

1. **Prepare the Eggs:** Slice the hard-boiled eggs in half and remove the yolks.
2. **Make the Filling:** Mash the yolks and mix with mayonnaise, Dijon mustard, pickle relish, salt, and pepper until smooth.
3. **Assemble:** Spoon or pipe the yolk mixture back into the egg whites.
4. **Garnish:** Sprinkle with a pinch of paprika.
5. **Serve:** Chill before serving.

Hummus and Pita Bread

Ingredients:

- 1 cup hummus (store-bought or homemade)
- 4 pita bread rounds
- Olive oil for drizzling (optional)
- Fresh parsley for garnish (optional)

Instructions:

1. **Prepare the Pita:** Cut the pita bread into wedges or triangles.
2. **Warm the Pita (Optional):** Lightly toast or warm the pita wedges in the oven or on a skillet.
3. **Serve:** Arrange the hummus in a bowl and serve with pita wedges. Drizzle with olive oil and garnish with parsley if desired.

Fruit Salad

Ingredients:

- 1 cup strawberries, sliced
- 1 cup pineapple, diced
- 1 cup grapes, halved
- 1 orange, peeled and segmented
- 1/2 cup blueberries
- 1/2 cup kiwi, peeled and sliced
- 1 tbsp honey (optional)
- Fresh mint leaves for garnish (optional)

Instructions:

1. **Prepare the Fruit:** Wash and chop the fruit into bite-sized pieces.
2. **Toss Together:** Combine all the prepared fruit in a large bowl.
3. **Optional Sweetening:** Drizzle with honey and toss gently to combine.
4. **Serve:** Garnish with fresh mint leaves and serve chilled.

Cheese and Charcuterie Board

Ingredients:

- 3 types of cheese (soft, hard, and semi-soft, e.g., Brie, Cheddar, Gouda)
- 3 types of charcuterie (e.g., prosciutto, salami, chorizo)
- Crackers or baguette slices
- Fresh fruits (e.g., grapes, figs, apple slices)
- Nuts (e.g., almonds, walnuts)
- Jam or honey for dipping

Instructions:

1. **Prepare the Board:** Arrange the cheeses and charcuterie on a large wooden board or platter.
2. **Add Accompaniments:** Fill in spaces with crackers, fruits, nuts, and small bowls of jam or honey.
3. **Serve:** Let guests enjoy creating their own combinations!

Quinoa Salad

Ingredients:

- 1 cup cooked quinoa (cooled)
- 1 cup cucumber, diced
- 1/2 cup cherry tomatoes, halved
- 1/4 cup red onion, finely chopped
- 1/4 cup fresh parsley, chopped
- 2 tbsp olive oil
- 1 tbsp lemon juice
- Salt and pepper, to taste

Instructions:

1. **Prepare the Salad:** In a large bowl, combine the cooked quinoa, cucumber, tomatoes, red onion, and parsley.
2. **Dress the Salad:** Drizzle with olive oil and lemon juice, then toss to combine.
3. **Serve:** Season with salt and pepper and serve chilled or at room temperature.

Antipasto Skewers

Ingredients:

- 12 small skewers or toothpicks
- 12 cherry tomatoes
- 12 mozzarella balls (bocconcini)
- 12 slices of salami or prosciutto
- 12 black olives
- Fresh basil leaves

Instructions:

1. **Assemble the Skewers:** Thread a cherry tomato, mozzarella ball, folded slice of salami, olive, and a fresh basil leaf onto each skewer.
2. **Serve:** Arrange the skewers on a platter and serve as an appetizer.

Tuna Salad Wraps

Ingredients:

- 1 can (5 oz) tuna, drained
- 2 tbsp mayonnaise
- 1 tbsp Dijon mustard
- 1/4 cup celery, finely chopped
- 1/4 cup red onion, finely chopped
- Salt and pepper, to taste
- 4 large whole-wheat wraps or tortillas
- Lettuce leaves

Instructions:

1. **Prepare the Tuna Salad:** In a bowl, mix the tuna with mayonnaise, Dijon mustard, celery, onion, salt, and pepper.
2. **Assemble the Wraps:** Lay a lettuce leaf on each tortilla, then spread the tuna salad mixture.
3. **Wrap and Serve:** Roll up the wraps tightly and slice them into halves or thirds. Serve immediately.

Watermelon Feta Salad

Ingredients:

- 4 cups watermelon, cubed
- 1 cup feta cheese, crumbled
- 1/4 cup red onion, thinly sliced
- 1/4 cup fresh mint, chopped
- 1 tbsp olive oil
- 1 tbsp balsamic glaze (optional)

Instructions:

1. **Prepare the Salad:** In a large bowl, combine watermelon, feta, red onion, and mint.
2. **Dress the Salad:** Drizzle with olive oil and optional balsamic glaze.
3. **Serve:** Toss gently to combine and serve chilled.

Shrimp Cocktail

Ingredients:

- 1 lb large shrimp, cooked and peeled
- 1/2 cup cocktail sauce
- 1 tbsp lemon juice
- Lemon wedges for garnish

Instructions:

1. **Prepare the Shrimp:** Arrange the cooked shrimp around a serving platter.
2. **Serve:** Place cocktail sauce in the center of the platter with lemon wedges. Serve immediately.

Cold Fried Chicken

Ingredients:

- 4 chicken pieces (drumsticks, thighs, or breasts)
- 1 cup buttermilk
- 1 cup all-purpose flour
- 1 tbsp paprika
- 1 tsp garlic powder
- 1 tsp onion powder
- Salt and pepper, to taste
- Vegetable oil for frying

Instructions:

1. **Marinate the Chicken:** Place the chicken pieces in a bowl and cover with buttermilk. Let it marinate for at least 2 hours in the refrigerator.
2. **Prepare the Breading:** In a separate bowl, combine flour, paprika, garlic powder, onion powder, salt, and pepper.
3. **Coat the Chicken:** Remove the chicken from the buttermilk, then dredge each piece in the flour mixture until well-coated.
4. **Fry the Chicken:** Heat oil in a large skillet over medium-high heat. Fry the chicken until golden brown and crispy, about 10-12 minutes per side. Drain on paper towels.
5. **Serve Cold:** Let the fried chicken cool to room temperature before serving. Enjoy!

Veggie Spring Rolls

Ingredients:

- 8 rice paper wrappers
- 1 cup shredded carrots
- 1 cup cucumber, julienned
- 1/2 cup red bell pepper, julienned
- 1/4 cup fresh cilantro leaves
- 1/4 cup fresh mint leaves
- 1/2 cup cooked vermicelli noodles (optional)
- Soy sauce or peanut dipping sauce for serving

Instructions:

1. **Prepare the Veggies:** Slice the vegetables and herbs into thin strips.
2. **Soften the Rice Paper:** Dip each rice paper wrapper into warm water for about 10-15 seconds until softened.
3. **Assemble the Rolls:** Lay the softened rice paper on a flat surface. Place a small amount of each veggie and some noodles (if using) in the center.
4. **Roll the Spring Rolls:** Fold in the sides and roll tightly. Repeat for the remaining wrappers.
5. **Serve:** Serve with soy sauce or peanut dipping sauce.

Pimento Cheese Spread

Ingredients:

- 8 oz cream cheese, softened
- 1 cup sharp cheddar cheese, shredded
- 1/2 cup mayonnaise
- 1/4 cup pimentos, chopped
- 1 tsp garlic powder
- Salt and pepper, to taste

Instructions:

1. **Combine the Ingredients:** In a mixing bowl, combine cream cheese, cheddar cheese, mayonnaise, pimentos, garlic powder, salt, and pepper.
2. **Mix Well:** Stir everything together until smooth and creamy.
3. **Serve:** Serve with crackers, vegetables, or spread on bread.

Cucumber Sandwiches

Ingredients:

- 1 cucumber, thinly sliced
- 1/2 cup cream cheese, softened
- 1 tbsp fresh dill, chopped
- 8 slices white or whole wheat bread
- Salt and pepper, to taste

Instructions:

1. **Prepare the Spread:** Mix cream cheese, dill, salt, and pepper in a bowl until smooth.
2. **Assemble the Sandwiches:** Spread the cream cheese mixture onto the bread slices. Layer with thin cucumber slices.
3. **Serve:** Cut the sandwiches into small squares or triangles and serve.

Tomato and Mozzarella Skewers

Ingredients:

- 1 pint cherry tomatoes
- 8 oz fresh mozzarella balls (bocconcini or ciliegine)
- Fresh basil leaves
- Balsamic vinegar for drizzling (optional)
- Olive oil for drizzling (optional)
- Salt and pepper, to taste

Instructions:

1. **Assemble the Skewers:** On small skewers or toothpicks, thread a cherry tomato, mozzarella ball, and basil leaf.
2. **Season:** Drizzle with olive oil and balsamic vinegar, then season with salt and pepper.
3. **Serve:** Serve immediately as a fresh appetizer.

Roasted Chickpeas

Ingredients:

- 1 can (15 oz) chickpeas, drained and rinsed
- 1 tbsp olive oil
- 1 tsp paprika
- 1/2 tsp garlic powder
- Salt and pepper, to taste

Instructions:

1. **Prepare the Chickpeas:** Pat the chickpeas dry with paper towels. Preheat the oven to 400°F (200°C).
2. **Season:** Toss the chickpeas with olive oil, paprika, garlic powder, salt, and pepper.
3. **Roast:** Spread the chickpeas on a baking sheet in a single layer and roast for 25-30 minutes, stirring halfway through.
4. **Serve:** Let cool slightly and enjoy!

Sweet Potato Salad

Ingredients:

- 2 medium sweet potatoes, peeled and cubed
- 1/2 red onion, finely chopped
- 1/4 cup olive oil
- 2 tbsp apple cider vinegar
- 1 tsp honey
- 1/2 tsp mustard
- Salt and pepper, to taste
- Fresh parsley, chopped (optional)

Instructions:

1. **Cook the Sweet Potatoes:** Boil or steam the cubed sweet potatoes until tender, about 10-12 minutes.
2. **Prepare the Dressing:** In a small bowl, whisk together olive oil, apple cider vinegar, honey, mustard, salt, and pepper.
3. **Assemble the Salad:** Toss the cooked sweet potatoes with the dressing and red onion. Garnish with fresh parsley.
4. **Serve:** Serve warm or chilled.

Mini BLT Sandwiches

Ingredients:

- 8 slices of bread (white, whole wheat, or brioche)
- 4 slices of bacon, cooked and halved
- 1 tomato, sliced
- Lettuce leaves
- Mayonnaise

Instructions:

1. **Prepare the Sandwiches:** Spread mayonnaise on the bread slices. Layer with lettuce, tomato slices, and bacon halves.
2. **Assemble:** Top with another slice of bread and cut into small squares or halves.
3. **Serve:** Serve as mini sandwiches for a perfect snack or appetizer.

Grilled Chicken Skewers

Ingredients:

- 2 chicken breasts, cut into bite-sized pieces
- 1 tbsp olive oil
- 1 tbsp lemon juice
- 1 tsp garlic powder
- 1 tsp paprika
- Salt and pepper, to taste

Instructions:

1. **Prepare the Marinade:** In a bowl, mix olive oil, lemon juice, garlic powder, paprika, salt, and pepper.
2. **Marinate the Chicken:** Coat the chicken pieces in the marinade and let sit for at least 30 minutes.
3. **Grill the Skewers:** Thread the chicken onto skewers and grill over medium heat for 5-7 minutes per side, until cooked through.
4. **Serve:** Serve with a dipping sauce or enjoy as-is.

Mediterranean Couscous Salad

Ingredients:

- 1 cup couscous
- 1 1/4 cups boiling water
- 1/2 cucumber, diced
- 1 cup cherry tomatoes, halved
- 1/4 red onion, finely chopped
- 1/2 cup kalamata olives, pitted and chopped
- 1/4 cup feta cheese, crumbled
- 2 tbsp olive oil
- 1 tbsp lemon juice
- 1 tbsp red wine vinegar
- Salt and pepper, to taste
- Fresh parsley, chopped (for garnish)

Instructions:

1. **Prepare the Couscous:** In a bowl, pour the boiling water over the couscous. Cover and let it sit for 5 minutes. Fluff with a fork to separate the grains.
2. **Assemble the Salad:** In a large mixing bowl, combine the couscous with cucumber, tomatoes, red onion, olives, and feta cheese.
3. **Dress the Salad:** In a small bowl, whisk together olive oil, lemon juice, red wine vinegar, salt, and pepper. Pour over the salad and toss to combine.
4. **Serve:** Garnish with fresh parsley and serve chilled.

Roasted Red Pepper Dip

Ingredients:

- 2 red bell peppers, roasted and peeled
- 1/2 cup Greek yogurt
- 1 tbsp olive oil
- 1 tbsp lemon juice
- 1 garlic clove, minced
- Salt and pepper, to taste
- Fresh parsley, chopped (for garnish)

Instructions:

1. **Roast the Peppers:** Roast the red peppers over an open flame or under a broiler until the skins are charred. Place them in a bowl and cover to steam. Peel off the skins, remove seeds, and chop.
2. **Blend the Dip:** In a food processor, combine the roasted peppers, Greek yogurt, olive oil, lemon juice, garlic, salt, and pepper. Blend until smooth.
3. **Serve:** Garnish with fresh parsley and serve with pita bread, crackers, or veggies.

Stuffed Mini Peppers

Ingredients:

- 12 mini bell peppers, tops cut off and seeds removed
- 1/2 cup cream cheese, softened
- 1/2 cup goat cheese, crumbled
- 1 tbsp fresh chives, chopped
- 1 tbsp fresh parsley, chopped
- 1 tsp garlic powder
- Salt and pepper, to taste

Instructions:

1. **Prepare the Filling:** In a bowl, mix the cream cheese, goat cheese, chives, parsley, garlic powder, salt, and pepper until well combined.
2. **Stuff the Peppers:** Carefully stuff each mini pepper with the cheese mixture.
3. **Serve:** Arrange the stuffed peppers on a platter and serve chilled or at room temperature.

Guacamole and Chips

Ingredients:

- 3 ripe avocados, peeled and pitted
- 1/2 red onion, finely chopped
- 1 tomato, chopped
- 1 tbsp lime juice
- 1 tbsp fresh cilantro, chopped
- 1 garlic clove, minced
- Salt and pepper, to taste
- Tortilla chips, for serving

Instructions:

1. **Mash the Avocados:** In a bowl, mash the avocados with a fork or potato masher until smooth but slightly chunky.
2. **Add the Veggies:** Stir in the red onion, tomato, lime juice, cilantro, and garlic.
3. **Season:** Add salt and pepper to taste.
4. **Serve:** Serve with tortilla chips for dipping.

Spinach and Cheese Stuffed Croissants

Ingredients:

- 1 package croissant dough (8 rolls)
- 1/2 cup cooked spinach, drained and chopped
- 1/2 cup ricotta cheese
- 1/4 cup mozzarella cheese, shredded
- 1 tbsp olive oil
- Salt and pepper, to taste

Instructions:

1. **Prepare the Filling:** In a bowl, combine the cooked spinach, ricotta cheese, mozzarella cheese, olive oil, salt, and pepper.
2. **Assemble the Croissants:** Unroll the croissant dough and place a spoonful of the spinach mixture on each dough triangle. Roll up the croissants as usual.
3. **Bake:** Place the croissants on a baking sheet and bake according to package instructions, usually 10-12 minutes, until golden brown.
4. **Serve:** Let cool slightly before serving.

Bacon-Wrapped Dates

Ingredients:

- 12 dates, pitted
- 12 slices bacon
- 1/4 cup goat cheese or blue cheese (optional)

Instructions:

1. **Prepare the Dates:** If using cheese, stuff each date with a small amount of cheese.
2. **Wrap the Dates:** Wrap each date with a slice of bacon and secure with a toothpick.
3. **Cook:** Place the bacon-wrapped dates on a baking sheet and bake at 375°F (190°C) for 15-20 minutes, or until the bacon is crispy.
4. **Serve:** Serve warm as an appetizer.

Cabbage Slaw

Ingredients:

- 1/2 small head of green cabbage, shredded
- 1/2 small head of purple cabbage, shredded
- 1 carrot, shredded
- 1/4 cup mayonnaise
- 1 tbsp apple cider vinegar
- 1 tbsp Dijon mustard
- Salt and pepper, to taste

Instructions:

1. **Prepare the Veggies:** In a large bowl, combine the shredded green and purple cabbage with the shredded carrot.
2. **Make the Dressing:** In a small bowl, whisk together mayonnaise, apple cider vinegar, Dijon mustard, salt, and pepper.
3. **Toss the Slaw:** Pour the dressing over the cabbage mixture and toss to combine.
4. **Serve:** Serve immediately or refrigerate for 30 minutes to chill before serving.

Corn on the Cob

Ingredients:

- 4 ears of corn, husked
- 4 tbsp butter
- Salt and pepper, to taste

Instructions:

1. **Boil the Corn:** Bring a large pot of water to a boil. Add the corn and cook for 8-10 minutes, until tender.
2. **Serve:** Remove the corn from the water, brush with butter, and season with salt and pepper.
3. **Serve:** Serve hot.

Veggie Wraps

Ingredients:

- 4 large flour tortillas
- 1 cup hummus
- 1/2 cucumber, thinly sliced
- 1/2 red bell pepper, thinly sliced
- 1 carrot, shredded
- 1/2 cup spinach leaves
- Salt and pepper, to taste

Instructions:

1. **Prepare the Veggies:** Slice the cucumber, red bell pepper, and shred the carrot.
2. **Assemble the Wraps:** Spread a thin layer of hummus on each tortilla. Layer with cucumber, bell pepper, carrot, and spinach leaves.
3. **Wrap and Serve:** Roll up the tortillas tightly and slice into smaller pieces for serving.

Grilled Cheese Sandwiches

Ingredients:

- 8 slices of bread (your choice)
- 4 tbsp butter, softened
- 4 slices of cheddar cheese (or your preferred cheese)
- 4 slices of mozzarella cheese (optional)

Instructions:

1. **Prepare the Sandwiches:** Butter one side of each slice of bread. Place a slice of cheddar and mozzarella cheese between two slices of bread, with the buttered sides facing out.
2. **Grill the Sandwiches:** Heat a skillet or griddle over medium heat. Place the sandwiches in the pan and cook for 3-4 minutes on each side, or until golden brown and the cheese is melted.
3. **Serve:** Cut the sandwiches in half and serve hot.

Fresh Bruschetta

Ingredients:

- 4 ripe tomatoes, chopped
- 1/4 cup fresh basil, chopped
- 2 tbsp extra virgin olive oil
- 1 tbsp balsamic vinegar
- 1 garlic clove, minced
- Salt and pepper, to taste
- 1 baguette, sliced and toasted

Instructions:

1. **Prepare the Topping:** In a bowl, combine the tomatoes, basil, olive oil, balsamic vinegar, garlic, salt, and pepper. Stir to combine.
2. **Toast the Bread:** Toast the baguette slices until they are golden and crispy.
3. **Assemble the Bruschetta:** Spoon the tomato mixture onto the toasted bread slices.
4. **Serve:** Serve immediately as an appetizer or side dish.

Chocolate Chip Cookies

Ingredients:

- 1 1/2 cups all-purpose flour
- 1/2 tsp baking soda
- 1/2 tsp salt
- 1/2 cup unsalted butter, softened
- 1/2 cup granulated sugar
- 1/2 cup packed brown sugar
- 1 tsp vanilla extract
- 1 large egg
- 1 1/2 cups semisweet chocolate chips

Instructions:

1. **Preheat Oven:** Preheat the oven to 350°F (175°C).
2. **Prepare the Dough:** In a medium bowl, whisk together the flour, baking soda, and salt. In a separate bowl, beat together the butter, granulated sugar, brown sugar, and vanilla extract until smooth. Add the egg and mix well. Gradually add the flour mixture, stirring until combined. Fold in the chocolate chips.
3. **Bake:** Drop spoonfuls of dough onto a lined baking sheet, spacing them about 2 inches apart. Bake for 8-10 minutes, or until the edges are golden.
4. **Serve:** Let the cookies cool on a wire rack before serving.

Lemon Bars

Ingredients:

- **For the crust:**
    - 1 cup all-purpose flour
    - 1/4 cup powdered sugar
    - 1/2 cup unsalted butter, softened
- **For the filling:**
    - 2 large eggs
    - 1 cup granulated sugar
    - 2 tbsp all-purpose flour
    - 1/4 tsp baking powder
    - 2 tbsp lemon juice
    - Zest of 1 lemon
    - Powdered sugar, for dusting

Instructions:

1. **Prepare the Crust:** Preheat the oven to 350°F (175°C). In a bowl, combine the flour and powdered sugar. Cut in the butter until the mixture is crumbly. Press into the bottom of a greased 9x9-inch baking dish. Bake for 15-20 minutes, until golden brown.
2. **Prepare the Filling:** In a bowl, whisk together the eggs, granulated sugar, flour, baking powder, lemon juice, and lemon zest. Pour over the baked crust.
3. **Bake:** Bake for 20-25 minutes, until the filling is set and slightly golden around the edges.
4. **Serve:** Let the bars cool completely before dusting with powdered sugar and cutting into squares.

Picnic-Style Potato Salad

Ingredients:

- 4 medium potatoes, peeled and cubed
- 1/2 cup mayonnaise
- 1/4 cup sour cream
- 1 tbsp Dijon mustard
- 1/4 red onion, finely chopped
- 1 celery stalk, chopped
- 1/4 cup pickles, chopped (optional)
- Salt and pepper, to taste
- 2 hard-boiled eggs, chopped
- Fresh parsley, chopped (for garnish)

Instructions:

1. **Cook the Potatoes:** Boil the potatoes in salted water for 10-12 minutes, or until fork-tender. Drain and let cool slightly.
2. **Make the Dressing:** In a bowl, mix together the mayonnaise, sour cream, Dijon mustard, red onion, celery, pickles, salt, and pepper.
3. **Assemble the Salad:** Toss the potatoes with the dressing until well coated. Gently fold in the chopped eggs.
4. **Serve:** Garnish with parsley and serve chilled.

Turkey and Cheese Roll-ups

Ingredients:

- 8 slices of deli turkey
- 4 slices of cheese (cheddar, Swiss, or your choice)
- 1/4 cup mayonnaise or mustard (optional)
- Fresh lettuce leaves (optional)

Instructions:

1. **Assemble the Roll-ups:** Lay a slice of cheese on top of each turkey slice. Add a small amount of mayonnaise or mustard if desired. Place a lettuce leaf on top (optional).
2. **Roll-up:** Roll the turkey and cheese slices tightly into a cylinder.
3. **Serve:** Slice the roll-ups into bite-sized pieces and serve as an appetizer or snack.

Sweet and Sour Meatballs

Ingredients:

- 1 lb ground beef or turkey
- 1/2 cup breadcrumbs
- 1/4 cup grated Parmesan cheese
- 1 egg
- 1/2 tsp garlic powder
- Salt and pepper, to taste
- 1 cup sweet and sour sauce

Instructions:

1. **Make the Meatballs:** In a bowl, mix together the ground beef, breadcrumbs, Parmesan cheese, egg, garlic powder, salt, and pepper. Shape into meatballs, about 1-inch in size.
2. **Cook the Meatballs:** Heat a large skillet over medium heat. Cook the meatballs for 8-10 minutes, turning them until browned and cooked through.
3. **Add the Sauce:** Pour the sweet and sour sauce over the cooked meatballs and stir to coat. Let the meatballs simmer in the sauce for 5 minutes.
4. **Serve:** Serve warm as an appetizer or side dish.

Marinated Olives

Ingredients:

- 2 cups mixed olives (green, black, Kalamata, etc.)
- 2 tbsp olive oil
- 1 tbsp red wine vinegar
- 1 garlic clove, minced
- 1 tsp dried oregano
- 1 tsp red pepper flakes (optional)
- 1 tbsp lemon zest
- Fresh parsley, chopped (for garnish)

Instructions:

1. **Prepare the Marinade:** In a bowl, combine the olive oil, red wine vinegar, garlic, oregano, red pepper flakes, and lemon zest.
2. **Marinate the Olives:** Add the olives to the bowl and stir to coat. Cover and refrigerate for at least 2 hours (overnight for best flavor).
3. **Serve:** Garnish with fresh parsley and serve chilled or at room temperature.

Fruit Tart

Ingredients:

- **For the crust:**
    - 1 1/2 cups all-purpose flour
    - 1/2 cup powdered sugar
    - 1/2 cup unsalted butter, softened
- **For the filling:**
    - 8 oz cream cheese, softened
    - 1/2 cup powdered sugar
    - 1/4 tsp vanilla extract
    - 1/2 cup heavy cream
- Fresh fruit (berries, kiwi, etc.)

Instructions:

1. **Prepare the Crust:** Preheat the oven to 350°F (175°C). In a bowl, combine the flour and powdered sugar. Cut in the butter until the mixture is crumbly. Press into the bottom of a tart pan. Bake for 10-12 minutes, or until golden.
2. **Make the Filling:** Beat together the cream cheese, powdered sugar, and vanilla extract until smooth. In a separate bowl, whip the heavy cream until stiff peaks form. Fold the whipped cream into the cream cheese mixture.
3. **Assemble the Tart:** Spread the cream filling into the baked crust. Top with fresh fruit.
4. **Serve:** Refrigerate the tart for at least 2 hours before serving.

Roasted Potato Wedges

Ingredients:

- 4 large potatoes, scrubbed and cut into wedges
- 2 tbsp olive oil
- 1 tsp garlic powder
- 1 tsp paprika
- 1/2 tsp dried thyme
- Salt and pepper, to taste
- Fresh parsley, chopped (for garnish)

Instructions:

1. **Preheat Oven:** Preheat the oven to 400°F (200°C).
2. **Season the Potatoes:** In a bowl, toss the potato wedges with olive oil, garlic powder, paprika, thyme, salt, and pepper until evenly coated.
3. **Roast the Potatoes:** Arrange the wedges in a single layer on a baking sheet. Roast for 30-35 minutes, flipping halfway through, until golden and crispy.
4. **Serve:** Garnish with chopped parsley and serve immediately.

Zucchini Fritters

Ingredients:

- 2 medium zucchinis, grated
- 1/2 cup all-purpose flour
- 1/4 cup grated Parmesan cheese
- 1 large egg
- 1/2 tsp garlic powder
- 1/2 tsp onion powder
- Salt and pepper, to taste
- 2 tbsp olive oil (for frying)
- Fresh parsley, chopped (for garnish)

Instructions:

1. **Prepare the Zucchini:** Place the grated zucchini in a clean kitchen towel and squeeze out any excess moisture.
2. **Make the Batter:** In a bowl, combine the zucchini, flour, Parmesan, egg, garlic powder, onion powder, salt, and pepper. Mix until well combined.
3. **Fry the Fritters:** Heat the olive oil in a skillet over medium heat. Spoon heaping tablespoons of the mixture into the skillet and flatten slightly. Fry for 3-4 minutes on each side, until golden and crispy.
4. **Serve:** Remove from the skillet and place on paper towels to drain. Garnish with fresh parsley and serve warm.

Sliced Cold Cuts and Pickles

Ingredients:

- 1/2 lb assorted cold cuts (salami, turkey, ham, etc.)
- 1/2 lb sliced cheese (Swiss, cheddar, provolone, etc.)
- 1 cup assorted pickles (dill, sweet, or bread and butter)

Instructions:

1. **Prepare the Platter:** Arrange the sliced cold cuts and cheese on a large platter.
2. **Add the Pickles:** Place the assorted pickles alongside the cold cuts and cheese.
3. **Serve:** Serve immediately as a snack, appetizer, or sandwich filler.

Roasted Cauliflower Salad

Ingredients:

- 1 medium cauliflower, cut into florets
- 2 tbsp olive oil
- 1/2 tsp turmeric
- 1/2 tsp cumin
- Salt and pepper, to taste
- 1/4 cup red onion, thinly sliced
- 1/4 cup pomegranate seeds (optional)
- 1/4 cup fresh cilantro, chopped
- 2 tbsp tahini dressing (optional)

Instructions:

1. **Preheat Oven:** Preheat the oven to 400°F (200°C).
2. **Roast the Cauliflower:** Toss the cauliflower florets with olive oil, turmeric, cumin, salt, and pepper. Spread them out on a baking sheet and roast for 25-30 minutes, or until tender and lightly browned.
3. **Assemble the Salad:** Let the cauliflower cool slightly before adding it to a bowl. Add red onion, pomegranate seeds, and fresh cilantro. Drizzle with tahini dressing, if desired.
4. **Serve:** Toss to combine and serve warm or at room temperature.

Mini Meatball Subs

Ingredients:

- 1 lb ground beef or turkey
- 1/4 cup breadcrumbs
- 1/4 cup grated Parmesan cheese
- 1 egg
- 1 tsp garlic powder
- 1/2 tsp dried oregano
- Salt and pepper, to taste
- 8 mini sub rolls
- 1 cup marinara sauce
- 1 cup shredded mozzarella cheese

Instructions:

1. **Make the Meatballs:** Preheat the oven to 375°F (190°C). In a bowl, mix together the ground meat, breadcrumbs, Parmesan, egg, garlic powder, oregano, salt, and pepper. Shape into small meatballs.
2. **Cook the Meatballs:** Place the meatballs on a baking sheet and bake for 15-20 minutes, or until cooked through.
3. **Assemble the Subs:** Slice the mini sub rolls and spoon marinara sauce into each roll. Place 2-3 meatballs in each sub and top with shredded mozzarella.
4. **Melt the Cheese:** Place the subs on a baking sheet and bake for 5-7 minutes, or until the cheese is melted and bubbly.
5. **Serve:** Serve immediately as a tasty snack or meal.

Spinach and Ricotta Puffs

Ingredients:

- 1 sheet puff pastry, thawed
- 1 cup cooked spinach, drained and chopped
- 1/2 cup ricotta cheese
- 1/4 cup grated Parmesan cheese
- 1/4 tsp nutmeg
- Salt and pepper, to taste
- 1 egg, beaten (for egg wash)

Instructions:

1. **Prepare the Filling:** In a bowl, combine the cooked spinach, ricotta, Parmesan, nutmeg, salt, and pepper. Mix until well combined.
2. **Prepare the Pastry:** Preheat the oven to 400°F (200°C). Roll out the puff pastry and cut it into squares. Place a spoonful of the spinach mixture in the center of each square.
3. **Fold and Seal:** Fold the pastry over the filling to form a triangle or rectangle. Press the edges to seal.
4. **Bake:** Brush the tops of the puffs with the beaten egg. Place them on a baking sheet and bake for 12-15 minutes, or until golden and puffed.
5. **Serve:** Serve warm as an appetizer or snack.

Cantaloupe and Prosciutto

Ingredients:

- 1 small cantaloupe, peeled and cut into bite-sized pieces
- 8 slices prosciutto, thinly sliced
- Fresh mint leaves (optional)

Instructions:

1. **Assemble the Dish:** Wrap a piece of prosciutto around each cantaloupe cube.
2. **Serve:** Arrange the wrapped cantaloupe and prosciutto on a platter. Garnish with fresh mint leaves, if desired, and serve immediately.

Brownie Bites

Ingredients:

- 1 box brownie mix (or homemade brownies)
- 2 tbsp vegetable oil (if using brownie mix)
- 1/4 cup water (if using brownie mix)
- 1 egg (if using brownie mix)

Instructions:

1. **Preheat Oven:** Preheat the oven to 350°F (175°C). Grease a mini muffin tin or line it with paper liners.
2. **Prepare the Brownie Batter:** Prepare the brownie batter according to the package instructions or your homemade recipe.
3. **Bake the Brownie Bites:** Spoon the brownie batter into the mini muffin tin, filling each cup about 3/4 full. Bake for 12-15 minutes, or until a toothpick inserted comes out clean.
4. **Serve:** Let the brownie bites cool before removing them from the tin. Serve as a bite-sized treat.

Sliced Brie and Grapes

Ingredients:

- 8 oz Brie cheese, sliced
- 1 cup grapes (red or green), halved

Instructions:

1. **Prepare the Platter:** Arrange the Brie cheese slices and halved grapes on a serving platter.
2. **Serve:** Serve immediately as a simple, elegant appetizer.

Iced Lemonade

Ingredients:

- 1 cup fresh lemon juice (about 4-6 lemons)
- 1/2 cup granulated sugar
- 4 cups cold water
- Ice cubes
- Lemon slices and mint leaves, for garnish

Instructions:

1. **Make the Lemonade:** In a pitcher, combine the fresh lemon juice and sugar. Stir until the sugar is dissolved.
2. **Add Water:** Pour in the cold water and stir well. Adjust sweetness by adding more sugar if desired.
3. **Serve:** Fill glasses with ice cubes and pour the lemonade over. Garnish with lemon slices and mint leaves, if desired.